HERMAN KLABER 'KING OF HOPS'

Julie McDonald Zander

ISBN 978-0-9846019-7-4

Cover photo of the *Titanic* from Dreamstime.com and Herman Klaber
photo courtesy of the Lewis County Historical Museum, P-9715.

ACKNOWLEDGMENTS

Special thanks to the Lewis County Historical Museum for providing access to historical photos, many of which were donated initially by Hazel Duncan.

I am grateful for information in newspaper articles and on historylink.org regarding Herman Klaber, the Boistfort Valley's 'King of Hops.'

The Chronicle in Centralia initially published an article I wrote marking the centennial of Herman Klaber's death in the Atlantic Ocean, where he perished along with 1,800 others aboard the White Star Company's new luxury liner, the RMS *Titanic*. Also reprinted here are public domain photos of the *Titanic*.

Thanks to Ray Zander, Larry Zander, Margaret Shields, and Edna Fund for proofreading the book. Marion Duckworth and Tracie Heskett also gave me suggestions to expand the story.

I hope you enjoy learning about the King of Hops who died April 15, 1912, after the "unsinkable" *Titanic* struck an iceberg and plunged to the bottom of the Atlantic Ocean.

Julie McDonald Zander

LIKE MANY GHOST TOWNS, the community of Klaber might have faded obscurely into the annals of history had it not been for the role it played in developing the hop industry in Washington and the tragic way in which its founder perished.

Today, 75 percent of the hops produced in the United States are grown in Washington, which is the nation's largest producer of hops. Now they're grown in the Yakima Valley, but it was in Western Washington where pioneer

Ezra Meeker first established hops farming in 1865. Meeker, who left Indiana and crossed the Oregon Trail in 1852 with his wife, Eliza Jane, eventually settled in the Puyallup Valley where in March 1865 he planted hop vine cuttings that his brother, Jacob, received from Olympia beer brewer Charles Wood. The plants flourished, and when his father earned more than $150 selling a single bale of hops weighing 180 pounds, Meeker recognized an opportunity to make money. In 1867 he planted four acres in hops and, the following year, built his first kiln to cure the key ingredient in beer near his cabin. Each year Meeker devoted more acreage to the crop and, by the early 1890s, he cultivated more than 500 acres in hops and harvested 400 tons a year.

Farmers throughout the region converted wheat fields to hops crops, and when the crop in England failed in 1882, prices soared to seventy cents a pound. Meeker earned half a million dollars a year selling bales of hops to the European markets, spending four years in London establishing a branch to market his hops worldwide. He also sold hops regionally, with Portland brewer Henry Weinhard a loyal customer.

Meeker published a book called *Hop Culture in the United States* in 1883 to help Washington hops farmers "avoid the mistakes of early pioneers." British newspapers quoted him as a hops expert, and he reigned as hops king of the world.[1]

Disaster struck in 1892, when Meeker noticed the hop foliage in a field near his office seemed off color and unnatural. Upon investigating, he spied a hops lice and discovered the entire field alive with millions of munching mites rav-

Lewis County Historical Museum P-5747

Herman Klaber bought property in the early 1900s for a hops farm in the Boistfort Valley of Lewis County. He constructed a manager's house, above, and kilns, seen below by a field in full bloom. Both photos donated by Hazel Duncan were taken circa 1912. A large hops cone is seen at right.

Wikimedia Commons

Lewis County Historical Museum P-5746

7

Photo from the sign at former hops farm site

In the photo above, letters on the dry kilns at the Klaber hops fields spelled out the name of the community. The photo below from Hazel Duncan's collection shows the approach to the Klaber hops yards in full bloom and the dry kilns in the background about 1912.

Lewis County Historical Museum P-5766

aging a once-healthy crop of hops. Farmers from British Columbia to California sold their crops for far less than anticipated, and Meeker's neighbors and other farmers who owed him more than $100,000 couldn't repay the debt.

"These people simply could not pay, and I forgave the debt, taking no judgments against them, and I have never regretted the action," Meeker wrote.[2] "All my accumulations were swept away, and I quit the business—or rather, the business quit me."

BIRTH OF A FUTURE HOPS KING

WHILE MEEKER WAS HIRING 1,000 PEOPLE to harvest his hops crops in Washington, a young boy born in California November 18, 1870, was learning the art of negotiation from his father, an immigrant from Austria who operated a post office and later became a coal dealer.

A young man with a thirst for adventure, George Klaber left his Austrian homeland for a new life in the United States and on October 6, 1848, at the age of twenty-three, proudly took an oath in New York to become a U.S. citizen.

Dreams of wealth likely lured him to the West during the 1849 Gold Rush, where he settled in Mokelumne Hill, which became one of California's richest and bawdiest gold mining towns. The population soared to 15,000 as people from many nations converged in a quest for gold. The town became the county seat in 1852. By 1860, the same year that George Klaber was appointed by the U.S. Senate to serve as deputy postmaster at Mokelumne Hill, miners had tapped out the gold fields and the population

KLABER HOP FIELDS 200 ACRES KLABER WASH.

Lewis County Historical Museum P-2532

The photos offers a view of the 200-acre Klaber hopfields, shed and hop house, used for drying hops.

dissipated. The county seat was moved to San Andreas in 1866. Today, fewer than 700 people live in the once-thriving town that they sometimes refer to as "Moke Hill."

Within a half dozen years, George Klaber moved farther west to San Francisco, where he established a business as a coal and wood dealer. The *1867 Great Register of San Francisco* listed his Bay Area business on Tehama Street. He and his wife, Bertha, who was born in Baden, Germany, raised two children—Sarah, born in 1869, and Herman, who arrived a year later.

A DEALER IN HOPS

AFTER COMPLETING HIS EDUCATION, young Herman Klaber found a job as clerk to hops merchant William Uhlmann & Co. of San Francisco and New York, one of the nation's largest hops-dealing companies. He entered the hops business just before Meeker quit.

Lewis County Historical Museum P-5795

Hazel Duncan's photo above shows the Klaber hopyard's Tent Row in 1912 with a long row of tents on the left and a long row of cabins on the right and hops crews between them. The field had eighty tents housing 1,500 people. Duncan's photo below shows a flatbed wagon loaded with bins filled with hops on the way to the No. 2 kiln in the Klaber hopyard.

Lewis County Historical Museum P-5801

Lewis County Historical Museum P-5751

The photo above from Hazel Duncan shows the main street of Klaber with a wagon being loaded in front of the flour and feed warehouse next to the Klaber Post Office. Below, a stagecoach stops outside the Klaber Post Office and store.

Photo on sign at hopyard site

While lice devastated the Washington crop in 1892, Klaber put an optimistic face on the disaster, as reported in the Puyallup Citizen. "Herman Klaber, of the Uhlmanns, estimates that 45,000 bales will be reached but the Citizen thinks Mr. Klaber's ideas too rosy, as the blossoms are confined to the upper portions of the poles and the vines do not interlace and bear arms draping down from the top of the poles in cascades of hop blossoms as they have generally done in previous years. This is probably due to the long, cold, wet spring which lasted far into the summer and so shorted the season that there has been little time for a normal development of the vine."[3]

Klaber traveled throughout the nation visiting hopfields and negotiating the purchase of hops. *The Auburn Argus*, a Seattle area newspaper, described Klaber in September 1897 as "the genial hop buyer who represents William Uhlmann & Co." He visited the Green River Valley to inspect hopyards and pronounced he could see no trace of lice. "Mr. Klaber has just returned from Yakima, and the newspaper quoted him as describing the Yakima hops as "generally good, but for yield he thinks the Green River district leads anything he ever saw." He said the price of hops wasn't expected to top ten cents, depending on the price overseas. "He thought that a jump in price from practically nothing to 10 cents was about all that could naturally be expected in one season."[4]

In the early 1890s, Klaber then joined with his cousin, Marcus J. Netter in San Francisco, and Max Wolf as business partners in Klaber, Wolf & Netter, hop dealers. The company had offices in London, San Francisco, Portland, and Tacoma.

In 1893, Klaber moved north, first to Puyallup and then to Tacoma, where he worked as a hops broker, owned a cigar store, and sold insurance. He also formed Herman Klaber & Co. and shared interest in Klaber Investment Co. with his brother-in-law, H.A. Kaufman, who later was proprietor of the St. Helens Hotel in Chehalis.

The Tacoma-based Herman Klaber and Co. bought thousands of pounds of hops from growers in Washington, Oregon, and California, and Herman Klaber often appeared in regional newspapers as a spokesman quoted under "Hop News." In March 1905, he warned Oregon hops growers that they risked losing the ability to sell hops to English markets if they failed to pack their product better. "We refer to the picking and packing of a large proportion of the Oregon crop this season in which a large quantity of leaves, stems, and other extraneous matter could be found."

He continued, "Our brewers in England object very much to this, and unless next year's crop is much better picked and handled, we can foresee that it will prejudice our buyers here against your Oregon hops....

"We have had no cause to complain of Washington hops the past season, and unless the growers are more careful, Washington's will no doubt find preference with our brewers."[5]

BUILDING A MODEL HOPS FARM

As A HOPS BROKER, Klaber traveled frequently, including to Lewis County, where farmers had been planting hops since the 1880s. The Henriot family on Cowlitz

Lewis County Historical Museum P-5797

The Hazel Duncan photo above shows wagons at the Klaber yard loaded with hops bins. Text on back of photo says "Dad and Mike on Cub, Bert Roundtree on Dan, O.D. and Frank Cassady, Agnes Novotne, and Mrs. A. George Dillon driving Shorty and Buck. Mr. Ritter is driving the mules, Maude and Jonah. Mr. Pickle is sitting on hop boxes in the third wagon." Below is the Boistfort Bridge, left, and the schoolhouse near the hopyard.

Photos from sign at hopyard site

Hazel Duncan's photo above shows Frank Pete with children on hops bin surrounded by vines, two full picking baskets in front of them, circa 1915. Below, an unidentified Indian man and woman sit on stools picking hops.

Prairie grew hops, as did farmers in Chehalis, Winlock, Mossyrock, Silver Creek, and other areas of the county. Children near hops farms started school late so the families could earn extra money picking hops during the month-long September season. Eventually hops covered 900 acres of the county.[6]

Through Klaber & Co., Herman Klaber in 1903 bought eighty acres in the Boistfort Valley from C.W. Maynard and started building a house, barn, and four model hop kilns.[7] Three years later, he purchased forty acres from John Roundtree and additional land from Lucy Ann Hogue, widow of homesteader John Hogue. He eventually owned 360 acres in the Boistfort Valley, aptly named for the French word meaning "small valley surrounded by green hills." He planted 200 acres of hops on the John Hogue donation land claim, creating the Northwest's largest single hopyard.

But it wasn't just a hopyard. Klaber invested $75,000 (equivalent to nearly $2 million today) to build a community that he initially thought of naming Klaberville but eventually called Klaber. Six towering chimneys on modern dry kilns spelled out the town's name—K L A B E R—with one letter per chimney, visible for miles around.

He hired contractors to erect a 920-square-foot building with a general merchandise store, blacksmith shop, post office, and meeting hall. J.O. Wallace managed the store, while barber H.L. Morris trimmed whiskers and locks in a shop of 168 square feet.

"Mr. Klaber has for many years recognized the attractiveness of Chehalis hops of which he has always been a heavy buyer," a newspaper reported.[8] "He expects to make the fame of 'Klaber's Chehalis Hops' worldwide in a few years."

Klaber invested time and money building a model hops farm in the pastoral valley settled in the 1850s. His family's two-story bungalow sat on a knoll overlooking the state's largest hopyard. The manager lived in a house with ten rooms and the assistant manager lived in a two-story home.[9] Klaber built five cottages for the help, each with five rooms, and tapped into a nearby spring and installed a $3,000 gravity water system with two reservoir tanks piping hot and cold water to the homes.

Some of the 1,000 or more pickers who arrived in early September—primarily Cowlitz and Chehalis Indians—pitched tents near the Chehalis River's south fork. Many others lived in the 400 wooden shacks Klaber erected in two rows, facing each other. Each twelve-foot-square shack had a wooden floor and a wood stove for heat and cooking. Spring-fed spigots near the shacks provided water.[10] Advertisements began appearing in local newspapers in early August seeking hop pickers for the "largest and best hopyard in Washington" with 200 acres operated by Herman Klaber & Co.

Pickers could earn three dollars a day filling 125-pound boxes with hops, which were then loaded onto wagons and drawn up ramps to well-ventilated drying floors on the second story of the twelve dry kilns. After hop cones were roasted, bleached, and baled, workers wrapped burlap around them for shipping and stored them in warehouses at the farm or trucked them to a large red depot at Ceres. The depot was along the Northern Pacific route between

Lewis County Historical Museum P-5791

The view in the Hazel Duncan photo above from the winter of 1912 shows the road along the Klaber hopyards and poles standing as far as the eye can see. Her photo below shows two unidentified men with a five-horse team tilling the soil at the hopyard.

Lewis County Historical Museum P-5756

Chehalis and Willapa Harbor.[11] The Klaber hopyard produced 1,500 bales a year, each weighing about 200 pounds.

For many workers, picking hops offered an opportunity to socialize and reconnect with people they hadn't seen for a year. Under sunny skies with warm weather, women and children often enjoyed the chance to visit and play while picking the cone-shaped hops from vines climbing twelve-foot-high poles. Evening entertainment included music and dancing in barns on the farm.[12]

Klaber put his negotiation skills to work in persuading government officials in April 1907 to rename the nearly half-century-old Boistfort post office to reflect his new town, Klaber.

Klaber, Wolf & Netter of Portland opened its London branch in May 1907 with H.E. Freeman stationed there as representative.[13] Klaber also continued as an advocate for hops growers and dealers, testifying before the House Ways and Means Committee in Washington, D.C., in November 1908 regarding proposed tariffs. The Portland hops dealer and E.S. Horst of San Francisco represented 3,600 hops growers in asking for a tariff of twenty-four cents a pound, claiming that the "hop industry is on its last legs."[14]

MARRIED IN 1907

WITH HIS PORTLAND GROCERY STORE, Tacoma investment company, frequent travels as a hops dealer, and founder of a new town, Klaber still found time to woo Gertrude G. Ginsberg, the daughter of Russian-born cigar store owner Samuel Ginsberg and his wife, Berthar, of Sacramento. She was born September 3, 1885, but didn't let the fifteen-year age difference deter her from marrying Klaber on February 13, 1907. The couple joined other newlyweds in honeymooning at the luxury Hotel Del Monte east of Monterey, California, a resort with polo grounds, golf course, parkland, gardens, and a race track.[15]

Wikimedia Commons

Above, the port side of the RMS Titanic on April 10, 1912, before it departed Southampton, England, on its fateful journey. At left is the grand staircase inside the luxury liner. Below is the fitness room for first-class passengers.

Wikipedia

http://vrienden.wordpress.com/2012/04/07/100-jaar-titanic/

Wikimedia Commons

Wikimedia commons

The top photo shows the Titanic, right, and its sister ship, the Olympic, side by side at Thomson Graving Dock in Belfast, Ireland. The lower photo shows Reading and Writing Room on the A-Deck aboard the Titanic.

After their marriage, the couple visited California frequently, but they shared their home in Tacoma with Klaber's widowed mother, Bertha; his widowed brother-in-law, H.A. Kaufman; and two nieces, Elsa Kaufman and Dorothy Danhauser. They also employed a live-in servant, Elisa Balsiger.

The Klabers later moved to Portland, where on February 8, 1910, Gertrude gave birth to a daughter, Bernice Janet Klaber. Although they lived in Portland, they spent summers at the Lewis County bungalow on what Klaber referred to as the "ranch."

A FATEFUL VOYAGE

THIS WAS THE LIFE KLABER LEFT BEHIND when he boarded the luxury passenger ship, the *Olympic*, for a three-month business trip to Europe seeking hops buyers. Before he left, the forty-one-year-old businessman met with an attorney and signed his last will and testament on January 11, 1912. Did Klaber have a premonition that he might never return to his wife and two-year-old daughter in Portland? Or perhaps he simply wanted to ensure that his considerable wealth would be distributed as he saw fit and ensure that if he died, he would be buried without any ostentation whatsoever. After stopping at the London office of Klaber, Wolf & Netter, he traveled the European continent drumming up buyers for his hops. After several months, though, he was ready to return home.

The "hops king" wrote to a business partner in Seattle, Ben Moyses of the Independent Brewing Company, shortly before heading home.

"I have determined to leave here for home on the new steamship *Titanic*. The other day I was sitting in a leading hotel here and noticed a man reading what looked like an American newspaper. I 'rubbered' over his shoulder and found that it was a copy of The Seattle Times. My, it looked good to me to see a Seattle newspaper here in London. I introduced myself and found that I was talking to a Seattle business man, W. R. Owens, and we spent five hours together talking about 'God's country.' I hope to be there soon and I shall leave here as soon as I can make arrangements."[16]

Herbert Edwin Freeman, London manager of Klaber, Wolf & Netter, accompanied Klaber to the offices of the White Star Line, seeing his wealthy boss purchase a first-class ticket for the maiden voyage of the RMS *Titanic*. It cost him 26 pounds 11 shillings (about $150 at the time). According to his ticket, No. 113028, he would be on the C deck in cabin C-124. Freeman later signed a deposition attesting to the purchase and saying he was with Klaber at London's Waterloo Station April 10 when the American boarded a special boat train for *Titanic* passengers leaving from Southampton.

Aboard the luxury ocean liner, Klaber shared a cabin with forty-year-old London stockbroker Austen Partner, who said goodbye to two sons at home before heading to Canada on business. Down the hall on the same deck were the cabins of John Jacob Astor, a New York property developer and great-grandson of the famous fur trader who founded Astoria, Oregon, and his entourage (his wife, a manservant, maid, private nurse, and a pet Airedale).

Dreamstime_xxl_19732503

The collage above depicts the sailing of the RMS Titanic, its collision with an iceberg, and the "unsinkable" luxury liner's plunge into the frigid waters of the Atlantic Ocean with survivors clustered in rowboats watching passengers perish.

Altogether, the ship carried more than 1,300 passengers and nearly 900 crew members.

Many were sleeping at midnight when they heard a grinding, tearing sound as forward motion of the ship halted and engines stopped. Men rapped on doors, awakening passengers and encouraging them to dress and climb to the top deck. One crew member told a woman the ship had only broken two pipes, but another advised her to board a lifeboat.

Passengers lucky enough to board lifeboats saw men lighting cigarettes and waving goodbye, musicians performing on the deck, and crew members scrambling to load the last lifeboats. At 2:17 a.m. April 15, the darkened hulk of the "unsinkable" luxury liner slipped into the frigid Atlantic Ocean, taking more than 1,500 people with her.

Most of the men aboard the *Titanic* died, but 705 men, women, and children survived on lifeboats.

RECOVERING FROM TRAGEDY

AFTER THE RESCUE OF SURVIVORS, searchers retrieved as many bodies as they could find to provide family members closure and allow them to bury their loved ones. David Netter, a liquor dealer with United Supply Co. of Philadelphia, sent a telegram followed by a letter asking about the body of his cousin, Herman Klaber. He described the hops king as six feet tall, with brown hair, a sandy complexion, a high forehead and straight nose, weighing about 190 pounds. He sent a photograph of his cousin, hoping his body could be identified.

Lewis County Historical Museum P-5736

Lewis County Historical Museum P-5752

The Hazel Duncan photo above shows ticket boss Mr. Brown, at center in the hop vines. Three-day-old colt Trilly nurses from its mother at the Klaber stables with an unidentified man nearby. Below, two men stand in an empty wagon.

Lewis County Historical Museum P-5754

Lewis County Historical Museum P-2353

Lewis County Historical Museum P-5761

Above, an Indian man picks hops with a baby buggy and children behind him. At left and below are trucks loaded with wrapped bales of dried hops ready for market circa 1912.

Lewis County Historical Museum P-5768

"Mr. Klaber's family has been reconciled to the fact that he has given up his life on the *Titanic*," Netter wrote May 8, 1912. "Naturally they desire me to use my best efforts as to any information concerning the remains that may be brought to shore."

His body was never identified among those recovered. He was listed among the wealthiest to perish on the *Titanic*. The Portland businessman owned two hop farms in Lewis County—the one at Klaber and another one-and-a-half miles southwest of Chehalis. He also owned a half interest in two businesses, the largest grocery store in Portland and Klaber, Wolf & Netter, a worldwide hops dealer. In addition, he owned Herman Klaber & Co. of Tacoma and a shared interest in Klaber Investment Co. of Tacoma with H.A. Kaufman.

Kaufman served as executor of his brother-in-law's will, which left most of his $500,000 estate to his wife and daughter, although he provided $25,000 each to his nieces, Dorothy Danhauser and Elsa Kaufman. Tragically, less than two years later, Dorothy was shot and killed by a former suitor, Abraham Pepper, while honeymooning in San Francisco with her husband, piano salesman S.L. Johnson. Elsa later married Seattle lawyer Sam Levinson.[17]

Klaber also gave $1,000 each to Freeman, the company's manager in London; stenographer Nellie Blade; and other employees. He also donated $1,000 each to the Beth Israel congregations in Tacoma and San Francisco, with the request that stained glass windows be installed to honor his late parents.

Lewis County Historical Museum P-5771

Above, a man and a boy work on the spraying cart in the Klaber hopfields. At right is a loaded hop truck. Below, in September 1911, workers have fun in the fields with Frank Casady pretending to arrest May Brown and Eva Knight.

Lewis County Historical Museum P-5764

Lewis County Historical Museum P-5753

After Herman's death, his wife asked that all of the family's personal effects at the Klaber hopyards be auctioned off as she didn't plan to live at Klaber again. Among the items sold was a motion picture outfit that Klaber had bought to provide entertainment for his pickers.[18]

Gertrude Klaber moved back to Sacramento to live with her parents. Although she was only twenty-six when her husband perished, she never remarried. She and her daughter lived in Sacramento with her father in 1920, but later moved into boarding houses and rental homes. Records show she traveled to Tokyo and Hawaii in the spring of 1956, when she was seventy. Gertrude Klaber died March 17, 1961, at San Francisco.

Their daughter, Bernice, grew up in California, traveled to Hawaii at the age of sixteen, and studied at the University of California at Berkeley in the early 1930s. She married attorney Samuel Jacobs, a Sacramento native, and the couple lived in San Francisco. Bernice died less than a year after her mother, on February 23, 1962, when she was fifty-two. Her husband passed away May 1, 1997. They had no children.

For two decades after the *Titanic* sank, workers continued harvesting hops at Klaber, but the crop was plagued by a downy mildew fungus. Without Herman Klaber to provide strong leadership, the hopyard floundered. World War I interrupted shipping of products to Europe, and Prohibition from 1920 to 1933 curtailed domestic demand for hops though the European market continued purchasing the product. Other setbacks followed when longtime Klaber hopyard superintendent Gus Anderson, a native of

These photos show the former site of the Klaber hopyard, marked by the historic sign erected by the Baw Faw Grange.

Photos by Julie McDonald Zander

Sweden, died in January 1936.[19] Then a fire in July 1940 destroyed a hop kiln, barn, and milk house at Klaber on property still owned by Gertrude Klaber but leased to J. Berkeley. Loss in the fire, of undetermined origin, was estimated at $10,000.[20]

By 1945, the hopyard closed and the community of Klaber faded away.

Today, only a sign erected by the Baw Faw Grange, next to Boistfort Elementary School, attests to the valley's former glory as the hop capital of the world. And Herman Klaber is enshrined in history as one of the 1,517 victims in a deadly maritime disaster.

END NOTES

[1] A tribute to Meeker, printed in *The Puyallup Press* on September 21, 1939, HistoryLink.org Essay 7742. Paula Becker, April 29, 2006.

[2] Ezra Meeker and Howard Driggs for Oregon Trail Memorial Association, *Covered Wagon Centennial and Ox-Team Days*, Yonkers-On-Hudson: World Book Company, 1932.

[3] *Syracuse Standard*, September 10,1897, Syracuse, New York.

[4] "Hop Notes," *The Mendocino Dispatch Democrat*, September 16,1892, Ukiah, California.

[5] *The Mendocino Dispatch Democrat*, March 17, 1905, Ukiah, California.

[6] Crowell, Sandra A. *The Land Called Lewis: A History of Lewis County, Washington*. Panesko Publishing. 2007.

[7] *The Centralia News-Examiner*, August 1903.

[8] *The Chehalis Bee-Nugget*, Dec. 21, 1906.

[9] *The Tacoma News*, Dec. 14, 1907.

[10] Kirk, Ruth, and Carmela Alexander. *Exploring Washington's Past*. University of Washington Press. 1990.

[11] Crowell, Sandra A. *The Land Called Lewis: A History of Lewis County, Washington*. Panesko Publishing. 2007.

[12] *Centralia Daily Chronicle*, Aug. 21, 1913.

[13] *The Morning Oregonian*, May 30, 1907.

[14] *The Galvaston Daily News*, Nov. 20, 1908.

[15] *Oakland Tribune*, Feb. 24, 1907.

[16] *The Seattle Times*, April 21, 1912.

[17] *Tacoma News Tribune*, April 12, 2001.

[18] *The Centralia Daily Chronicle*, Sept. 24, 1928.

[19] *The Chehalis Bee Nugget*, Jan. 10, 1936.

[20] *The Daily Chronicle*, July 20, 1955.

BIBLIOGRAPHY

"15 Years Ago: From *The Daily Chronicle* September 24, 1913," *The Centralia Daily Chronicle*, Sept. 24, 1928.

"20 Years Ago: *Chehalis-Bee Nugget*, Aug. 15, '12," *The Chehalis Bee Nugget*, Aug. 19, 1932.

"50 Years Ago: August 20, 1912," *The Daily Chronicle*, Aug. 20, 1962.

"50 Years Ago: October 17, 1912," *The Daily Chronicle*, Oct. 17, 1962.

"At Del Monte," *Oakland Tribune*, Feb. 24, 1907.

"The Auburn Argus says:" *Syracuse Standard*, September 10, 1897, Syracuse, New York.

Becker, Paula. "Ezra Meeker plants hops in the Puyallup valley in March 1865," HistoryLink.org, Essay 7742. April 29, 2006.

"Conditions of the Hop Market," *The Mendocino Dispatch Democrat*, Aug. 13, 1909.

Craker, Craig. "Washington State Tops When it Comes to Hops," *The Tri-City Herald*, September 21, 2012.

Crowell, Sandra A. *The Land Called Lewis: A History of Lewis County, Washington*, Panesko Publishing. 2007.

"Fine Weather Brings Hops Into Blossom," *The Centralia Daily Chronicle*, Aug. 21, 1913.

"First Cabin List on Doomed Ship," *The (Newcastle) Evening Chronicle*, April 16, 1912.

"For Lower Duty on Lemons," *The New York Times*, Nov. 20, 1908.

"Gus Anderson, Klaber Farmer, Dies Saturday," *The Chehalis Bee Nugget*, Jan. 10, 1936.

"Herman Klaber, representing Wm. Uhlmann & Co.," *The Mendocino Dispatch Democrat*, September 16, 1892, Ukiah, California.

"Herman Klaber, the well-known Tacoma hop man," *The Chehalis Bee-Nugget*, 1905.

"Hop Conditions Are Improving," *The Mendocino Dispatch Democrat*, June 26, 1908.

"Hop Growing in Washington," website http://www.usahops.org/index.cfm?fuseaction=hop_farming&pageID=13

"Hop louse invades Washington, Oregon, and British Columbia in 1892," HistoryLink.org Essay 2889.

"Hop News," *The Mendocino Dispatch Democrat*, March 17, 1905.

"Hop Notes," *The Mendocino Dispatch Democrat*, September 16, 1892, Ukiah, California.

"Hoping Against Hope for People's Safety," *The Titusville Morning Herald*, April 16, 1912.

Kirk, Ruth, and Carmela Alexander. *Exploring Washington's Past*. University of Washington Press. 1990.

"Klaber and the *Titanic*," *The Daily Chronicle*, March 11, 1972.

MacCracken, Gordon. "Boistfort site hops on register," *The Daily Chronicle*, June 18, 1977.

Martin, John. "Historical section awakens dozing memories of readers," *The Daily Chronicle Weekender*, July 10, 1976.

Meeker, Ezra, and Howard Driggs for Oregon Trail Memorial Association, *Covered Wagon Centennial and Ox-Team Days* (Yonkers-On-Hudson: World Book Company, 1932).

"Millionaire Hop Grower," *The Washington Post*, April 16, 1912.

"Oregon Hops Will Invade European Countries," *The Morning Oregonian*, May 30, 1907.

"Pacific Coast Passengers' Fate Remains Mystery," *The Centralia Weekly Chronicle*, April 17, 1912.

Ramsey, Guy Reed. *Postmarked Washington: Lewis and Cowlitz Counties*, Lewis County Historical Society. 1978.

"The Record of the Lost," *The Manitoba Free Press*, Winnipeg, April 19, 1912.

"Tariff Tinkers Hear Many Men Complain," *The Galvaston Daily News*, Nov. 20, 1908.

"*Titanic* Widow Is Killed By Suitor," *Trenton Evening News*, Feb. 26, 1914. (This story actually referred to Herman Klaber's niece.)

"*Titanic* Widow Killed by a Former Suitor," *Logansport Pharos-Reporter*, Feb. 24, 1914. (This story actually referred to Herman Klaber's niece.)

"Traders All Over Country Interested in Durst Project," *The Sunday Oregonian*, February 18, 1906.

"Wanted Hop Pickers" advertisements, *The Centralia Daily Chronicle*, Aug. 4, 1911; Aug. 5, 1911; Aug. 9, 1911; August 10, 1911; August 11, 1911; Aug. 18, 1911; Aug. 19, 1911; Aug. 21, 1911; Aug. 22, 1911; Aug. 3, 1912; Aug. 6, 1912; Aug. 14, 1912; Aug. 16, 1912; Aug. 17, 1912; Aug. 21, 1912; Aug. 22, 1912; Aug. 24, 1912; Aug. 25, 1912; Aug. 26, 1912; Aug. 29, 1912; Aug. 31, 1912; Aug. 21, 1913.

"Will File Klaber Will for Probate," *The Centralia Daily Chronicle*, May 2, 1912.

"Yesteryears: 15 Years Ago from *The Daily Chronicle* July 20, 1940," *The Daily Chronicle*, July 20, 1955.

Zander, Larry. "Klaber Valley once hop capital," *The Daily Chronicle*, Bicentennial Edition, July 1976.

Zander, Larry. "The Time Machine: Sept. 5, 1900: Klaber was once 'hop capital'," *The Daily Chronicle*, Sept. 5, 1975.

HERMAN KLABER 'KING OF HOPS'

CPSIA information can be obtained
at www.ICGtesting.com
Printed in the USA
LVOW03s0539170517
534668LV00030B/1332/P